IRA & 401k INCOME BUILDER

A Guide To Increasing Your Income Through Real Estate, Mortgage Notes, And Private Lending... Using Self Directed Retirement Plans

Randall Rodenhouse, PhD

Wasteland Press
www.wastelandpress.net
Shelbyville, KY USA

IRA & 401k Income Builder:
A Guide To Increasing Your Income
Through Real Estate, Mortgage Notes,
And Private Lending Using
Self Directed Retirement Plans
by Randall Rodenhouse, PhD

First Printing – August 2017
ISBN: 978-1-68111-197-1

Printed in the U.S.A.

0 1 2 3 4

CONTENTS

FOREWORD

Most people are highly dependent on the stock market for their retirement savings and have little to no control over their financial future. They don't understand what they are investing in and just hope for the best. I was the same way and at one point I decided that I needed to take control of my financial future. I found that investing in assets I understood and had interest in would positively reflect in my return.

I knew that to really grow my retirement, I needed to reduce my "consumption" of stocks and mutual funds and focus on high yielding alternative assets like real estate, mortgage notes, and private lending – just to name a few. This book "IRA Income Builder" is all about increase your awareness of the many alternative asset investment choices in a properly setup and executed IRA or 401k. You too can consistently grow your retirement tax free using a government sponsored savings plan tailored to you and your retirement needs.

As I started researching which government sponsored savings plan (IRA, SEP, SIMPLE, 401k, etc) was best for me, I soon realized the information available was very scattered and there was no real single source that clearly spelled out all of the different retirement plans. Therefore, I spent several months researching these plans and have condensed my findings in this book.

IraIncomeBuilder.com

INTRODUCTION

What Is Alternative Asset Investing?

If you read the headlines and listen to the news you would think the world is coming to an end. Constant babble about how the economy is bad, unemployment is high, the cost of daily necessities such as food/clothing/gas are only going up, and that people are not saving enough for retirement.

Although many of these things are true at the surface, there are things you can control and actively participate in by educating yourself and getting a different perspective. One of those "things" is your retirement plan. When most people hear the words "retirement plan" they immediately think of stocks, bonds, mutual funds and CDs. They think of the 401k at their employer or an IRA and don't feel like they have any control over the outcome of the retirement plans performance, even though they have chosen their own investments. Rightfully, most people think they just have to hope for the best since they really can't do much about how the stock market performs and they only have a limited selection of investment choices.

Well, I am here to say that the time for letting some unknown fund manager do the work for you is over. Most investors have a growing disillusionment of big financial Wall Street institutions and are looking to take control.

Remember it is *your money, your future and your plan*. You need to invest in alternative assets!

American's hold a vast majority of their money in stocks, bonds and mutual funds and in the recent financial crisis all three of these asset classes have lost value at the same time. Many individual investors and even some money management professionals think that it may be quite awhile before these financial assets deliver the kind of steady, reliable growth that they have in the past. It may not even happen in our lifetime, it is hard to tell.

All markets have cycles and at times they are booming and other times they go bust. In order to offset some of these swings, it is important that you put a portion of your money in alternative assets such as real estate, notes, private loans, tax liens, precious metals, commodities, oil/gas, receivables, small business, private equity investments, startup companies, etc. This is true diversification in contrast to diversifying into different securities which is NOT diversification at all (unlike what most financial planners tell you).

Get Inspired

Most startup companies are initially funded by private placements and many times the startup capital is originated from someone's retirement account. In fact, some of the great tech companies that you read about such as Google, PayPal, eBay, and Facebook were initially privately financed by angel investors and many of those investments may have been funded by someone's IRA or 401k. As those companies grew to the giants they are today, many of these smart investors would have seen fantastic appreciation and growth in their retirement account tax free.

In my opinion, you need to find investments that appeal to you based on your interest, experience and knowledge and those that meet your financial goals and risk tolerance. Everyone is different and there are plenty of opportunities to find high yielding investments.

Tax Protected Investing

No one likes to pay taxes, but many people invest and forego the opportunity to reduce their tax bill by utilizing government sponsored savings plans outlined in this book. No matter what you invest in, you will always come out better when you make your investments in a tax deferred or tax free retirement plan. These plans are designed to help you live better in retirement and are pretty easy to setup. The time spent will be well worth the effort.

Take the Time to Get Educated

You really need to take the time to get educated about self directed investing and all the potential investment choices. This will help you be more confident and take action when an opportunity presents itself. There are so many ways to invest and get a better return than in the traditional type assets and I am not talking about just in a down market. Some of my favorite investments are real estate, private loans, mortgage notes, tax liens and commodities (gold, silver, grains, oil, etc). I know real estate alone can conservatively return your retirement account double and even triple digit returns when done correctly.

Real Life Examples

I want to get you excited by showing you some recent examples of alternative assets I personally purchased in my Self Directed IRA and Solo 401k. I constantly wonder why people are so "stuck" on only buying stocks and bonds and don't even consider investing in real estate, notes, private lending, tax liens, gold and so on. I know that once people see the potential returns and the relatively low risk as compared to the traditional assets they will switch into alternative assets. Let's look at three examples - a real estate purchase, a note purchase and a private loan.

Real Estate Purchase

I purchased a single family home in South Carolina and after doing some cosmetic repairs, the property was rented for a total of 9 months before the tenants purchased the property for $120,000. This resulted in a cash-on-cash annual return of 36%. Even if I had not been able to sell the property and I had to continue renting the property the return would have been a strong double digit return.

Purchase price:	$91,000
Repairs:	$5,100
Rental profit:	$10,755 (9 months)
Sales price:	$120,000
Sales profit:	$23,900
Annual return:	36%

How hard is it to do such a deal? Not hard at all. In fact, this is a below average deal for me. Even so most people are not making these returns in their IRA or 401k and doing it consistently.

Discounted Mortgage Note Purchase

I purchased a first lien mortgage note on a single family property in South Carolina which was several payments behind. The note was purchased for $60,000 and had a $165,000 payoff (UPB + arrears, etc). The loan was modified to a UPB of $135,000 ($30,000 principal reduction) and a payment of $1298/month. The property value was $140,000 which gives a low investment to value (ITV) of 43% and very secure position. The note has a great yield and a possible bigger payday in the future.

Note price:	$60,000
Payoff:	$165,000
Modified UPB:	$135,000
ITV:	43%
Payment:	$1298/month
Annual yield:	25.8%

The yield would go up dramatically (over 100%) if the borrower refinances in a year and pays off the $135,000 loan. If the borrower continues to pay with the above loan terms the yield is 25.8%. Either way, I really don't care since my returns are stellar!

Private Loan

I met a real estate investor who wanted to buy, fix and flip a residential property but needed funding for the deal. The investor had a purchase agreement for $36,000 and the ARV was $79,000. The property needed about $14,000 in repairs. I agreed to lend around $29,000 (a very safe position) at 15% and 5 points upfront. The loan was repaid in 6 months which equates to an annualized return of 25%.

Property value:	$79,000
Purchase price:	$36,000
Loan amount:	$29,000
LTV:	37%
Interest rate:	15%
Points:	5%
Term:	6 months
Annual return:	25% (12.5% in 6 months)

I really hope that these examples and high returns inspire you to go out and think big for your retirement savings plan.

Why Have A 401k Or IRA?

Did you know that the Social Security Administration's trustee report stated that Social Security will begin to run a negative cash flow by the year 2017 and by the year 2036 will not be able to pay full benefits?

With the impending Social Security crisis and dramatic reduction in pensions, it is imperative to begin planning for your financial future today.

Social security might not be enough to secure your financial future. That's why the government created the different retirement savings plans, to help you save for your future. IRA and 401k investments grow tax free or tax deferred and compounds over time which maximizes your ability to grow wealth. There are many advantages (see A-E below) to these plans and the advantages will depend in part on the plan itself.

A. **Compound Interest**– Albert Einstein once said that "compound interest is the most powerful force on earth". This is because compound interest occurs when you not only earn interest on your original investment sum, but also on the interest earned on the original sum.

Let's look at a simple example of the power of compound interest. Let's say at age 25 you decide to cut out your daily coffee routine at the local coffee shop saving you $4.50 a day. That would equate to a little over $136 per month. If you received 8% in compounding interest each year, you would have $25,533 after 10 years. So after 20 years, you'd receive $80,658 and after 40 years when you are age 65, you'd have an amazing $456,602 (see graph).

This is a simple way to discipline yourself to invest in your retirement without giving up all the luxuries in life to get there. This is just one example of a simple way you can save and grow your wealth.

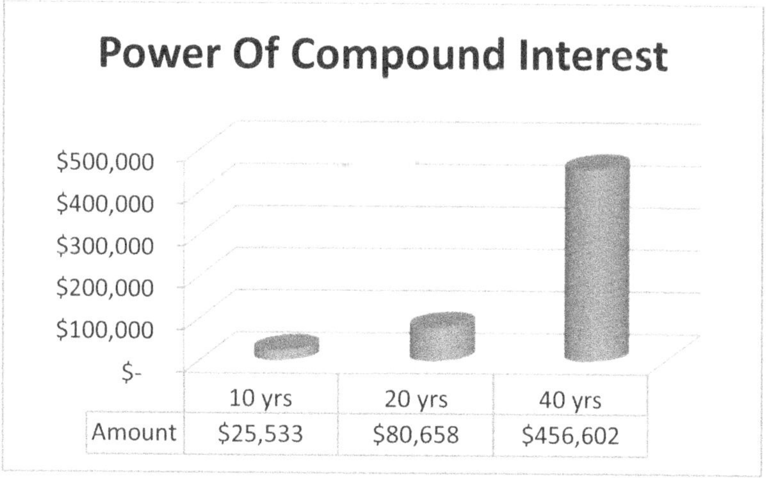

B. **Tax Deferred and Tax Free Profits** - This great power of compound interest is increased dramatically in tax advantage accounts such as IRAs and 401ks since the tax free or tax deferred portion also grows each year.

For example, if you were to contribute $5,000 a year to a tax advantaged account like an IRA or 401k and assume an 8% compound interest rate of return for

30 years, your bank account would be worth $561,416 at the end of year 30.

If you made the same investment in a non-tax sheltered environment (a fully taxable account), assuming a 28% tax rate, it would be worth $373,985 instead of $561,416. This is a whopping difference of $187,431. As you can see, in the graph below, the effect of taxes on your savings can be dramatic.

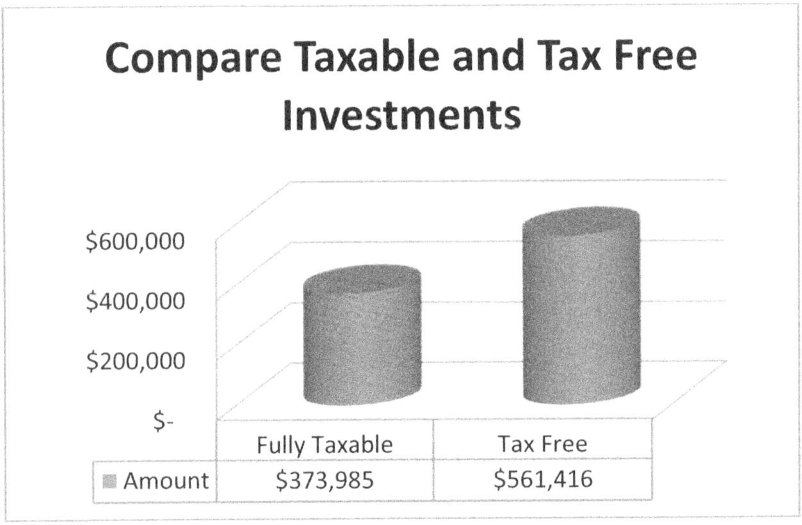

C. **Tax Deductions** - Certain IRAs and 401ks allow you to reduce your taxable income today while saving for your future. For example, if you contributed $5,500 to a Traditional IRA this year, and if you meet qualified income levels, you are eligible for a $5,500 tax deduction when filing your tax return. In a

401k, you can deduct up to $18,000 in 2016 and up to $24,000 if the plan allows the $6,000 catch up contribution.

D. **Protected from Creditors** - IRAs and 401ks are afforded protection from bankruptcy through the Employee Retirement Income Securities Act (ERISA) under the US Department of Labor and thus generally are shielded from creditors in bankruptcy proceedings.

E. **Wealth For Future Generations** – Some types of government sponsored savings plans allow the passing of assets to beneficiaries after death while avoiding taxes. This benefits your family's financial future by leaving valuable assets to your loved ones without the burden of taxes. This has been under some scrutiny recently since the government is trying to generate revenues in the current economic downturn.

In this book, I will explain the different types of individual and small business government sponsored savings plans. Each plan possesses unique tax advantages to maximize your future wealth and each has unique eligibility requirements. It is important that you figure out the right plan for you and start saving in order that you may enjoy the benefits of your retirement years.

This book will focus mainly on the various government sponsored *tax free savings plans*. In summary, chapters 1-5 will focus on government sponsored individual savings plans and chapters 6-9 will focus on government sponsored small business savings plans. Finally, chapters 10-11 will focus on government sponsored health and education savings plans.

Individual Plans

Chapter 1: Self Directed Traditional IRA

Self Directed IRAs are not special types of IRAs but follow the same set of rules and regulations as normal IRAs. Many people hear the term "self directed" and start to think that this is a special new plan by the government. In reality, the IRS does not even recognize the self directed IRA as a separate type of IRA but instead considers it just an IRA. Any IRA, whether it be a Traditional, Roth, SEP, SIMPLE can be "self directed". The term "self directed" is used to signify the ability of that IRA owner to make 100% of the investment decisions and not be limited to the typical employer type asset classes such as stocks, bonds and mutual funds. Instead, a properly setup self directed IRA with an appropriate custodian can invest in any of the IRS allowed investments of which there are numerous.

The Internal Revenue Service requires an independent third party to take care of all the IRA administration and cash flow of the account.

Typically, when dealing with traditional securities brokers like the Vanguard, Fidelity and Charles Schwab types, they can handle the administration as well as the purchase of stocks, bonds and mutual funds. However, for many investments outside this arena (like Forex and Futures for example) these companies are only able to handle the trading aspect but not the IRA administration aspect. And when we talk about investing in other alternative assets (i.e. real estate, notes, gold, etc) these traditional brokers are not setup at all to handle such transactions. This is where the self directed custodian is important (see the resources area for a list of some custodians).

Below is an extensive list (but not a comprehensive list) of the many alternative assets that you can invest in and put the gains directly into your IRA tax deferred or tax free. This list is not just for the traditional IRA but also for any "self directed" plan whether it be a Roth, Traditional, SEP, SIMPLE, CESA, HSA or even a solo 401k, all of which we will discuss in upcoming chapters.

Real Estate

- ✓ Residential Real Estate
- ✓ Commercial Real Estate
- ✓ Apartment Buildings
- ✓ Raw Land
- ✓ Tax Liens/Tax Deeds

Promissory Notes

- ✓ Mortgage/Deed of Trust Notes
- ✓ Secured Notes
- ✓ Unsecured Notes
- ✓ Car Paper
- ✓ Commercial Paper
- ✓ Factoring (accounts receivable)

Commodities and Currencies

- ✓ Energy - Oil/Gas
- ✓ Precious Metals - Gold/Silver
- ✓ Grains
- ✓ Forex (**For**eign **Ex**change or currency trading)
- ✓ Livestock
- ✓ Timber
- ✓ And Many More

Business

- ✓ Judgments/Structured Settlements
- ✓ Equipment Leasing
- ✓ Limited Liability Companies
- ✓ C-Corporations
- ✓ Limited Partnerships
- ✓ Private Placements
- ✓ Stock Offerings

Plus, many more...

The Traditional IRA was created in 1974 and is a great way to invest pre-tax dollars into your retirement account, grow them tax deferred and get an immediate tax deduction on the amount contributed depending on whether you or your spouse are covered by a retirement plan at work and your adjusted gross income. See the "Deductible Limits" table in this chapter.

Eligibility Requirements

- You and/or your spouse receive taxable compensation during the year.
- You were not age 70 ½ by the end of the year.

If both spouses have compensation and fit the age limit, then you can both contribute to a SEPARATE Traditional IRA. You cannot both contribute to the same IRA. In addition, you can contribute to a Traditional IRA if you currently have a compensation plan at work (like a 401k for example). Compensation is defined as the wages, salaries, commissions, bonuses, alimony and any other amount that you receive for providing personal services. Self employed individuals sometimes use the term "earned income" instead of compensation. Passive income such as interest, dividends and most rental income are not considered compensation for the purpose of funding an IRA.

One exception to the requirement of having earned income is a Spousal IRA. The truth is that the IRS makes an exception for married couples that want to boost their household retirement savings while providing a stay at home spouse the ability to build a nest egg. This arrangement is often referred to as a Spousal IRA. There are eligibility requirements for these Spousal IRAs.

Are You Eligible For A Spousal IRA?

Many households have an arrangement in which one spouse stays at home to care for the home and children. In such cases, if you are the stay at home parent, you can open an IRA in your name. In fact, the Spousal IRA is just a regular IRA. The name merely refers to the fact that the working spouse can make a contribution to an IRA held in the name of a non-working spouse.

The eligibility requirements for the Spousal IRA are straightforward:

Marital Status: Married
Tax Filing Status: Married, filing jointly
Earnings: Contributing spouse must have compensation/earned income that amounts to at least the amount annually contributed to the non-working spouse's IRA. If the contributing spouse also has an IRA, annual compensation/earned income

must exceed the combined contributions the IRAs. *Age*: The non-working spouse must be under 70 1/2 in the year of the contribution for a Traditional IRA. There are no age restrictions on a Roth IRA for a non-working spouse.

Once you determine that you meet the eligibility requirements, it is possible for you to open an IRA in your name and have your working spouse contribute to it. Understand that IRAs must be held separately, not jointly. This means that the non-working spouse owns the assets in the IRA.

Deductible Limits

A. If Covered By a Retirement Plan At Work

2016 Traditional IRA AGI Deduction Limits

Filing Status	Full Deduction	Phase Out*	No Deduction
Single or head of household	$61,000 or less	$61,000 - $71,000	$71,000 or more
Married filing jointly	$98,000 or less	$98,000 - $118,000	$118,000 or more
Married filing separately		Less than $10,000	$10,000 or more

*Phase Out – refers to partial deduction

B. If NOT Covered By A Retirement Plan At Work

2016 Traditional IRA AGI Deduction Limits

Filing Status	Full Deduction	Phase Out*	No Deduction
Single, head of household	No Limit	No Limit	No Limit
Married filing jointly or separately (spouse not covered)	No Limit	No Limit	No Limit
Married filing jointly (spouse covered)	$184,000 or less	$184,000 - $194,000	$194,000 or more
Married filing separately (spouse covered)		Less than $10,000	$10,000 or more

*Phase Out – refers to partial deduction

Contribution Limits

Unlike the Roth IRA which you will read about in the next chapter, the Traditional IRA has no income limits on contributions. For 2016 the standard contribution is $5,500 and for people 50 or older it is $6,500 ($1000 catch up contribution). These limits were the same in 2015.

The government gathers inflation statistics and uses that information to update the IRA contribution limits for the following year. Usually, the IRS releases this information in late October or early November.

Advantages

- Contributions are tax deductible (in full or partially)
- Taxes on earnings in the IRA are deferred
- If retiring at a lower tax bracket, you will be taxed at a lower rate.
  (Note: I believe taxes will go up in the future to pay for the wars and the large amounts of government spending so don't bank on a lower tax rate)

Withdrawals

The minimum withdrawal begins at age 70 ½ for a Traditional IRA or you will be faced with penalties. You are eligible to begin making withdrawals as early as 59 ½ without penalty. If you decide to withdraw money from your Traditional IRA account prior to the attainment of age 59½ you may be assessed an additional 10% early distribution penalty.

What Are The Exceptions To The 10% Early Distribution Penalty?

- You are receiving distributions in the form of an annuity.
- Beneficiary of a deceased IRA owner
- Disability (unable to work)
- Unreimbursed medical expenses that exceed 7.5% of your adjusted gross income
- Medical insurance premiums if unemployed
- Qualified higher education expense of the IRA owner, spouse and/or children
- Expenses associated with buying or building a first home ($10,000 limit)
- Payment of any IRS levy
- Qualified distribution for anyone in the reserves like the Army Reserve, National Guard, Naval Reserve, Air Force Reserve, etc.
- Rollover to another qualified plan

The list above does not include all the details, conditions and requirements necessary to receive a penalty free distribution from your IRA. Please consult with a tax professional for details.

Rules and Prohibited Transactions

See Chapter 3 for all the Rules and Regulations pertaining to IRA investing.

Chapter 2:
Self Directed Roth IRA

After many years of investing and successfully making hundreds of thousands of dollars, I became somewhat discouraged. Why? I was tired of sending a large portion of my profits to the IRS for taxes and I knew there had to be a better way. At the time I was investing outside a government sponsored savings plan. I would think to myself "how many more deals could I have done if I was not splitting my profits with the government because of taxes". I then started to study and research ways of keeping more of "my" money and now I am sharing these ideas and concepts with you. I found that Roth IRAs are a great way to grow your wealth income tax free and a Self Directed Roth IRA allows you to invest in almost anything including my favorites, real estate, mortgage notes and private lending.

Many people would prefer to forgo a tax deduction now in order to never have to pay taxes when you withdrawal the funds later. The main difference between the Traditional IRA discussed in Chapter 1 and the Roth IRA is that with the Roth IRA you contribute after tax dollars to the plan whereas with the Traditional IRA you contribute pre-tax dollars.

Yes, This Is Legal

I know by this time you are starting to think to yourself can I really buy real estate and gold in my IRA. The answer is YES! Don't let anybody tell you different. Most investors are not aware that such an opportunity exists because most IRA custodians do not offer truly Self Directed IRAs that allow you to invest in non-traditional assets like real estate, private loans, notes, tax liens, gold, oil, foreign exchange, factoring, and many more. If you ask your custodian or trustee and they say they never heard of that or "you can't do that", this just means that their company does not allow it since they only offer stocks, bonds and mutual funds or maybe CD products. A few possible custodians for Self Directed IRA type plans are listed in the resources area. Remember, there are other government sponsored savings plans if you are self employed which will be discussed in Chapters 6-9 of this book.

A Little Roth IRA History

Senator William Roth of Delaware was the chief legislative sponsor and the Roth IRA was established in 1997 by the Taxpayer Relief Act. Only the Traditional IRA existed before 1997 which was focused on granting tax breaks for money put into the plan. The Roth IRA focuses on tax breaks on the money withdrawn from the plan during retirement. This is a very important distinction. In a Roth IRA, you pay taxes on the "seed" and not the "crop". For example, let's say you invested $1 and grew it to a million dollars. In a Traditional IRA, you would pay taxes on the million dollars – the crop. In a Roth IRA, you would pay taxes on the $1 - the seed (and NOT on the one million dollars).

Imagine only paying taxes on the money going into the plan and leveraging this money to make $30,000 from a real estate transaction and not having to pay any taxes and being able to use all the money again on the next great deal. This is the greatest government gift but most people don't take advantage of these plans.

Eligibility Requirements

- No age requirement as long as your MAGI (Modified Adjusted Gross Income) is within allowable limits.
- You must meet the income limit requirements in order to contribute. The income limits

change almost every year and are shown below for 2016.

2016 Roth IRA Income Limits

Filing Status	Full Contribution	Contribution Phased Out	No Contributions
Single Filers	$117,000 or less	$117,000 - $132,000	$132,000 or more
Joint filers	$184,000 or less	$184,000 - $194,000	$194,000 or more

Contribution Limits

Year 2016: $5,500 Standard Contribution and $6,500 with catch up (age 50+)

As stated before, every year this number can be different since the government gathers inflation statistics and uses that information to update the IRA contribution limits for the following year. Usually, the IRS releases this information in late October or early November.

Withdrawals

Unlike the Traditional IRA, the Roth IRA has an advantage that there are no required withdrawals at any age. You can wait to pull your money out at 90 years old if you like or never pull it out at all. The contributions can be withdrawn at any age - tax and penalty free! Finally, the earnings portion in the account may be withdrawn tax and penalty free as long as it has been open for at least 5 years and you are over 59 ½ years of age.

Compare and Contrast Roth IRA versus Traditional IRA

All the information below is for the tax year 2016. Please note that these numbers change each year so consult with your CPA for updates. Earned income in the table below means all wages, salary, and tips you receive as an employee. Passive income like interest, dividends and rental income for the most part are not used to calculate eligibility and funding. Again, consult your CPA or tax professional for details.

	Roth	**Traditional**
What is it?	Government sponsored savings plan that gives tax advantages for individuals to save money for retirement by contributing post-tax dollars.	Government sponsored savings plan that gives tax advantages for individuals to save money for retirement by contributing pre-tax dollars.

Contribution Limits?	Up to $5,500 of earned income plus $1000 if age 50+. Contribution limits are reduced by amount put in another IRA.	Up to $5,500 of earned income plus $1000 if age 50+. Contribution limits are reduced by amount put in another IRA.
Who is eligible?	You must have earned income and MAGI less than $132,000 for single and $194,000 for a married couple in order to contribute to the plan.	You must be under 70 ½ and have earned income in order to contribute to plan.
Advantages?	Account grows tax free and the funds can be withdrawn tax free at age 59 ½ if the account has been open for at least 5 years.	Account grows tax deferred until the funds are withdrawn (and then they are taxed at your ordinary income rate).
Tax Deductible?	No	Yes.
Age Limit For Contributions?	No limits	70 ½
Distribution Requirements?	None	Must make minimum withdrawals at age 70 ½.

Withdrawal Penalties?	10% penalty for withdrawals before 59 ½, however contributions can be taken out any time.	10% penalty for withdrawals before 59 ½.

Chapter 3
IRA Rules and Regulations

Since the inception of the IRA in 1974, investing in alternative assets was allowed by the IRS and completely legal. Over the past several years, buying these alternative asset classes has become more popular due to the uncertainty in the stock market and the economic uncertainty in the world economy. People found that they did not want to limit their investments just to stocks, bonds and mutual funds. People are seeing a lot more opportunity in these alternative investments and that *Wall Street's* idea of diversification was false and very dangerous. Diversification into the same asset class is not diversification at all. When the stock market came crashing down it did not care about your diversification efforts and your entire portfolio (small cap, mid cap, large cap, financial, healthcare, services, technology, consumer goods, etc) was affected.

The Internal Revenue Code section 408 (IRC 408) states what investments are prohibited and all other types of investments are permitted as long as the IRS rules governing retirement plans are followed (i.e. no prohibited transactions). In general, an IRA cannot invest in collectibles and life insurance. See below for a partial list of prohibited investments.

Investments Not Permitted In Self Directed IRA

- Life Insurance
- Collectibles
  - ✓ Artwork
  - ✓ Antiques
  - ✓ Rugs
  - ✓ Automobiles
  - ✓ Gems
  - ✓ Stamps
  - ✓ Coins
  - ✓ Alcoholic Beverages
  - ✓ Metals

The exception to coin investing is that your IRA can invest in one, one-half, one quarter, or one tenth ounce US gold coins or one ounce silver coins minted by the Treasury Department. Certain platinum coins are permitted as well. Your IRA can also invest in certain gold, silver, platinum, palladium bullion.

In addition, you cannot invest your IRA in S Corporations. S Corporations do not allow IRAs as investors; they only allow individuals as investors.

Therefore, it isn't so much that IRAs are prohibited from investing in S Corporations rather that S Corporations don't permit having an IRA as a shareholder.

Allowable investments are summarized in Chapter 1; however the list of alternative investment options keeps growing as investors find areas where they have expertise and interest. Renewable energy and things like grain cars are definitely ideas to think about for the future. Speaking of grains, one entrepreneur decided to invest in a vodka distillery. He invested about $300,000 of his IRA funds and three years later his stake in the company grew to approximately $1.2 million. Now that is a fantastic return!

Why Is This Not More Popular And How Come I Never Heard About It Before?

The main reason it is not more popular is simply an economic one. There is typically more financial incentive for Wall Street to sell mutual funds and stocks since the fees are larger and there is more turnover in the products. Mutual funds, insurance companies and securities broker's make money when you buy their products and they are not interested in you buying a property and sitting on it for several years. Also, the cost of operations are higher for processing transactions like a real estate than for processing a typical stock purchase which results in lower profits. Most banks and brokers are limited by the types of investments they can offer and therefore you need to find a custodian that can help you.

The self directed plan types are not limited to just the Traditional and Roth IRAs. There are other government sponsored retirement plans which allow alternative asset investing if properly setup and structured. The list below will be discussed in upcoming chapters.

- SEP (Simplified Employee Pension)
- SIMPLE (Savings Investment Match Plan For Employees)
- Solo 401k
- HSA (Health Savings Account)
- CESA (Coverdell Education Savings Plan)

Rules and Prohibited Transactions

All the rules and restrictions are outlined in the IRS Publication 590 and IRC 4975. Not following these rules set forth for IRAs could affect the tax status of your account and could result in disqualification of the account and severe tax consequences.

Everything in the IRA has to be an arm's length transaction which means you as the IRA owner can't benefit from the asset owned by the IRA. You should always remember that the IRA is intended for your future retirement and not for you to benefit now. Therefore, you must always be asking yourself if there is any personal benefit for you now in doing such a transaction.

In general, prohibited transactions are any improper use of your IRA account by you, your beneficiary or any disqualified person.

Here are a few examples of prohibited transactions:

- Borrowing money from your IRA
- Selling property you already own to your IRA
- Receiving compensation for managing the IRA
- Using your IRA for security on a loan
- Buying property for personal use with IRA funds – i.e. personally using IRA property for a residence, office, vacation home, etc.

It is also important to remember that the IRA has to be a closed loop in terms of expenses and income or profit. The expenses related to the property must be paid from the IRA directly and all the income/profits be paid directly to the IRA as well. For example, if your IRA owns a rental property then all the rent must be returned directly to the IRA and all the expenses such as maintenance, insurance, taxes, etc must be paid directly from the IRA. In addition, you do not want to work on the property yourself since this is considered a contribution to your IRA and is not allowed.

Who Are Disqualified Persons?

They are you, your IRA holder, your spouse, parents, children and their spouses, grand children, grandparents and great grandparents, grandchildren and great grandchildren and their spouses. Also, anyone acting as a fiduciary and service provider of the IRA like your attorney, CPA or financial advisor. The weird thing is that brothers and sisters are not included as a disqualified person (but I personally would not take a chance since they are family).

Who Is Considered A Fiduciary?

The custodian of the IRA would be one. Anyone who provides investment advice for your IRA for a fee would be another. Anyone who has discretionary authority or control in managing your IRA or disposing of its assets would also be considered a fiduciary.

What Happens When My IRA Engages In A Prohibited Transaction?

1. The account stops being an IRA as of the first day of that year in which it occurred.
2. The account is treated as if all assets were distributed to you at their fair market value on the first day of the year.
3. If the total of those values is more than the basis in the IRA, you will have a taxable gain that is included in your income.

Chapter 4:
Self Directed IRA LLC

I just want to state up front that this plan which you will see advertised online by many companies is very appealing but you must get great legal and tax advice before starting such a plan. There is a lot of controversy surrounding these “checkbook” IRA plans and you must work with a qualified tax attorney to setup and administer. There are many grey areas and you are running a fine line with being non-compliant with the IRS rules if you don’t know exactly what you are doing.

These plans are promoted to help expedite your transaction since you do not have to go through a custodian to write a check to buy an asset or get paperwork signed, etc. The account owner manages the LLC and therefore can execute the transaction on the LLC level without the involvement of the IRA custodian, thus reducing fees and eliminating custodian transaction costs and delays.

I wanted to explain the concept and if you decide to go this route, you should work with tax professionals and ERISA attorneys that understand the laws and the details of these plans.

The Concept

The Self Directed IRA LLC structure has become a choice for gaining total investment control ("checkbook control") over your IRA funds and making investments tax free or tax deferred. This process has to be done carefully and setup by a professional tax attorney with advice from an experienced CPA. The concept of using an entity owned by an IRA to make an investment was first reviewed by the Tax Court in Swanson V. Commissioner 106 T.C. 76 in 1996. In the Swanson case, the tax court said that the funding of a new entity by an IRA for self-directing assets was a permitted transaction and not prohibited pursuant to Code Section 4975. The Swanson Case was later affirmed by the IRS in Field Service Advice Memorandum FSA 200128011. However, many disagree on the validity of the court case and many controversial discussions around this case study continue to be seen on financial blogs and forums.

How It Works

A new limited liability company (LLC) is established that is owned by the IRA account and managed by the IRA account holder. The IRA holder's funds are then transferred by the Custodian to the LLC's bank account providing the IRA holder with "checkbook control" over his or her IRA funds.

A Self Directed IRA LLC is made up of either a Traditional IRA or a Roth IRA and a "special purpose" Limited Liability Company. The account owner has complete control over the investments and sufficient flexibility to make investments without waiting on a signature or funds from the custodian. In addition, the cost of operations is lower versus attempting to operate out of a custodian account.

The LLC business entity is governed under the laws of the state in which the LLC is to be operated and is formed by filing Articles of Organization with that state like any other LLC. Once the IRA is moved inside the LLC, this allows the manager which is normally the IRA holder to setup a checking account which will be utilized for making allowed investments. The manager of the LLC can enter into contracts and agreements on behalf of the LLC. For example, in a real estate investment, the manager can make an offer and negotiate the deal and workout the closing details with the Title Company or with an Attorney. Once the property is acquired, the Manager can appoint a property manager to manage the property. In addition, there is asset protection as well in the IRA account through the use of an IRA LLC when it is setup properly.

Steps Involved

Step #1: Transfer funds to passive custodian for non-traditional investments (i.e. self directed IRA)

Step #2: Custodian invests IRA funds into new LLC. IRA account now owns LLC and you serve as manager (or a third party).

Step #3: Manager of the LLC directs LLC to purchase the asset. All income and gains go back to IRA tax free or tax deferred.

Simultaneously to the formation of the special purpose LLC, the retirement funds (whether in a IRA, SEP, SIMPLE, 401(k), 403(b), etc) will be transferred tax free from the current Custodian to a new FDIC backed/IRS approved passive Custodian that allows for truly Self Directed IRA investments, such as real estate. With a Self Directed IRA Checkbook structure you no longer have to pay excessive custodian fees based on account value and transaction fees. Instead a FDIC backed IRS approved passive custodian is used.

Once the IRA funds have been transferred to the new IRA Passive Custodian, the IRA Passive Custodian will then transfer the retirement funds tax free to the special purpose IRA LLC bank account. Once the IRA funds have been transferred tax free to the new IRA LLC bank account, the manager of the Self Directed IRA LLC (i.e. you) will have the authority to make investment on behalf of your IRA LLC. The Investment must be made in the name of your Self Directed IRA LLC. All income and gains generated by your IRA LLC will flow back to the IRA tax-free.

This setup allows for you to make investments quickly since you have the power to simply write a check or wire funds straight from you Self Directed IRA LLC bank account for a potential investment opportunity. This eliminates the delays associated with going through a custodian where you need to get approvals, funds and the proper signatures, etc for your investments.

Advantages of IRA LLC

- Unlimited Investment Options
- Investments Do Not Have To Be Approved By The Custodian
- True Checkbook Control
- Direct Access To Retirement Funds
- Limited Liability

- Low Annual Account Fees
- No Transaction Fees
- Bankruptcy Protection

Disadvantages to IRA LLC

There are some disadvantages of having a "checkbook" control IRA LLC. For one, the time and money to setup a LLC and continue to pay the state fees are pretty substantial and never ends until LLC dissolved. Second, it is not always crystal clear whether a particular asset or transaction is allowed or not. It comes down to interpretation of the IRS rules and your risk tolerance. Retirement plans are setup to benefit the retirement account and not the retirement owner directly. The custodian is a way to satisfy this arrangement and act as a buffer. When an IRA invests in a single member LLC that is managed by the account holder, you may get IRS scrutiny due to the nature of the arrangement. Therefore, you have to be extremely careful to act in the interest of your IRA only.

- Higher Probability Of Financial Penalties
- Potential Issue With IRS Not Allowing "Sweat Equity"
- Recordkeeping Burden
- Additional Funding Issue If LLC Needs Money

I think in the future the IRS will come out with some rules which will clearly define what you can and cannot do. For now, if you decide to go down this path, make sure you are working with a real tax expert and CPA with experience in this area.

Chapter 5: 403b Plans Explained

For the sake of completion, I wanted to include an overview of 403b plans. It is possible to have a Self Directed 403b plan, but unfortunately most schools, colleges and tax exempt organizations do not have alternative asset investing as part of their retirement plan. However, you can roll your 403b into a Self Directed IRA when you leave your employer or retire. A few employers even allow you to roll part or all of your funds from your 403b plan while you are still working.

Many people have a general understanding of what a 401k or IRA plan is and how it is used to help us save towards retirement. But what exactly is a 403b plan (also known as a tax sheltered annuity plan) and how is it different? A 403b plan is a retirement plan for employees of certain public schools, colleges, universities, and tax-exempt organizations, as well as certain ministers. A 403b plan is similar to a 401k plan in that contributions are tax deferred and tax deductible. Therefore, the funds are taxed when they are withdrawn from the account. For a Roth

403b, the contributions are after tax and earnings are tax free if they are part of a qualified distribution.

403b accounts for individuals can be the following types:

- Custodial account invested in traditional and non-traditional asset funds
- Annuity contract provided through an insurance company
- Retirement income account for church employees

Advantages of a Self Directed 403b Plan

- No income tax paid on allowable contributions until after withdrawals are made (usually after retirement). Allowable contributions either excluded or deducted from your income. NOTE: This benefit does not apply to contributions made to a Roth contribution program – income tax must be paid on contributions to the plan, but distributions from the plan are not taxed (assuming that certain requirements are met).
- Earnings and gains on amounts in your 403b are not taxed until withdrawal. Earnings on amounts in a Roth contribution program are tax free if your withdrawals are qualified

distributions. Otherwise, they are taxed upon withdrawal.

- You may be eligible to accept a credit for elective deferrals contributed to your 403b account.

Who Can Participate?

- Employees of tax exempt groups under section 501(c)(3) of Internal Revenue Code
- Public school employees involved in day-to-day operations of a school
- Employees of cooperative hospital service institutions
- Uniformed Services University of the Health Sciences (USUHS) civilian faculty and staff
- Employees of public school systems organized by Native American tribal governments
- Certain ministers are eligible

Who Can Set It Up?

Only employers can set up 403b accounts for their workers. A self-employed minister cannot set up a 403b for himself; only the organization with which the self-employed are associated can set it up.

Contribution Limits

Limits apply to how much can be contributed to your 403b every year. Penalties may accrue for exceeding the contribution limits.

For 2016, if you contribute the maximum basic salary deferral limit, and you qualify for both of the catch-up provisions listed below, you can potentially contribute up to $27,000 to your 403b:

- 2016 Elective Deferral Limit: $18,000.
- 403b Lifetime Catch-up: Only for employees with 15 or more years of service may be eligible to defer up to an additional $3,000.
- Age 50+ Catch-up: If 50 years old or older, you may be eligible to defer up to an additional $6,000 in 2016.

Total 2016 contribution limit on combined employee/employer contributions is 100% of your compensation or $53,000, whichever number is lower.

The problem with most 403b plans is that they are not very diverse and limited to mutual funds and annuities. With the modifications made to IRA plans over the years, 403b plans just don't compare. In a Self Directed IRA there is even more diversity and 100% control over your investments. For instance, with Self Directed IRAs you can invest in real estate, tax liens and other asset classes other than stocks and bonds.

With a typical 403b plan there is an 'investment adviser' who decides when and where to invest your money, keeping a large portion of the profits for themselves. In a Self Directed IRA the custodian listens to what the IRA owner wants and acts on it. And better yet, if this IRA is used for real estate investing, for example, the money is tax deferred or tax free and the entire gain can be used for another investment.

Yes, rolling over your 403b plan to a Self Directed IRA might be a little bit more work on your part at first, but once it is set up you will be happy with the many options available to you. Another option is to roll your 403b into a solo 401k if you meet the solo 401k requirements outlined in Chapter 6.

Again, all these limits change every year, so take the time to sit down with an expert tax attorney and CPA who specializes in this area.

Small Business Plans

Chapter 6: Solo 401k

The Solo 401k plan is for self employed individuals and many times referred to as Individual K or Solo K. Just to give you a historical perspective, in 1974 the IRA was created from a federal law called ERISA (Employee Retirement Income Security Act) which sets the standards for retirement accounts. Then in 1981 the 401k was introduced formally by the IRS. The Solo 401k plan is simply a traditional 401k plan covering only one employee and has become more popular as a result of the EGTRRA (Economic Growth and Tax Relief Reconciliation Act) tax law change that became effective in 2001. Essentially, EGTRRA law changed how salary deferral contributions are treated when calculating the maximum deduction limits for contributions to a 401k plan. This change created an opportunity for some people to put away additional amounts toward their retirement.

A Solo 401k is perfect for the sole proprietor such an independent contractor, consultant, real estate investor or any small business with no full time employees. The business can be a LLC, C-Corp, partnership or sole proprietorship. The solo 401k is a cost effective and tax efficient plan with more benefits than a Self Directed IRA.

Solo 401k Eligibility

To be eligible to benefit from a Solo 401k you need to have *self employment activity* and *no full time employees*.

- Self Employment Activity – This includes ownership and operation of a LLC, C-Corp, S Corp, partnership or sole proprietor where the business intends to turn a profit and contribute to the plan.
- Profit – There is no written number for how much profit the business must make or how much money must be contributed to the plan or even the timing. If you have a legitimate business and you intend to make profits you should be OK. The self employment activity does not have to be full time, in fact you can work another full time job with another employer and participate in their 401k plan at the same time. However, you cannot "double dip" and the contribution limit is from both elective deferral plans combined.
- No Full Time Employees – You must not have full time employees. You can have

independent contractors, employees under 21 years old and employees that work less than 1000 hours.

The solo 401k offers a variety of advantages over the Self Directed IRA such as:

- **Higher Contribution Limits.** In 2016, IRA allows only $5,500 and an additional $1,000 catch up provision (age 50+) whereas the Solo 401k allows an annual contribution limit of $53,000 with an additional $6,000 catch up provision (age 50+) and the same amount for the spouse that generates compensation from the business. Therefore, together you can contribute up to $106,000 or $118,000 if you are over age 50 and you have sufficient earned income. In addition, the Solo 401k plan contains a Roth account portion which can be contributed to *without income limits* (in Chapter 2 we discussed the Roth IRA income limits).

- **Loan Feature.** You can borrow funds from your Solo 401k up to $50,000 or 50% of the balance (whichever is smaller) for any reason and pay your 401k back at a low interest rate typically prime rate or prime plus 1%. The funds can be used for any purpose.

- **Total Control of Allowable Investment Choices.** Since you are trustee of the Solo 401k plan, you will be able to invest in almost any type of investment that suits you as long as it is allowed. Making an investment with your Solo 401k Plan is as simple as writing a check. As trustee of the Solo 401k Plan, you will have total control over your retirement assets to make real estate and other investments without custodian consent.

- **Reduced Fees.** Making an investment in your Solo 401k is as easy as writing a check and does not require you to get permission or have funds wired or mailed from a custodian which allows you to eliminate the expenses associated with this type of activity. This also allows you to act quickly when you find a great investment and need to move fast to take advantage of the opportunity.

- **UDFI Exemption.** If you buy real estate in an IRA and use some funds from your IRA and the remaining portion of the funds from non-recourse debt financing, typically you would incur UDFI (Unrelated Debt Financed Income) which is a type of UBTI (Unrelated Business Taxable Income) on which taxes must be paid. In a Solo 401k, you are not subject to the UDFI rules and the UBTI tax (which is high since it is based on trust tax rates).

Solo 401k plans can accept most rollovers from IRAs, other 401ks, 403b, SIMPLE, etc. The only exception is that a Roth IRA cannot be rolled into a Solo 401k plan.

Steps To Create Solo 401k Plan

Step #1: Business with no full time employees establishes IRS compliant Solo 401k plan based on your investment and retirement objectives.

Step #2: You open a bank account at a bank or credit union under the Solo 401k plan.

Step #3: Retirement funds are transferred from current custodian/trustee to new 401k bank account tax free.

Step #4: You as trustee can direct the Solo 401k plan to invest in alternative assets like real estate, notes, precious metals, tax liens, private lending, etc.

Salary Deferral and Profit Sharing Contributions

Above we discussed the higher contribution limits of the Solo 401k versus the IRA. Here I would like to discuss the details of salary deferral and profit sharing contribution for each of the different types of business structures.

C Corporation or S Corporation

Salary deferral contribution to a Solo 401k in 2016 is 100% of W-2 earnings up to the maximum of $18,000 or $24,000 if age 50 or older. For the profit sharing contribution the Internal Revenue Code Section 401(a)(3) states that the amount of employer contributions is limited to 25 percent of the compensation paid. Accordingly, a profit sharing contribution up to 25% of W-2 earnings can be contributed into a Solo 401k. In other words, the employer profit sharing contribution must be based on the compensation paid by the company to the employee, not the overall profits earned by the company.

Multiple Member LLC or Partnership

Salary deferral contribution to a Solo 401k in 2016 is 100% of the owner's self employment earnings up to the maximum of $18,000 or $24,000 if age 50 or older. For the profit sharing contribution the 25%

employer contribution amount is based on the income attributable to self-employment earnings, not necessarily the overall income of the entity since there are passive types of investments (i.e. rental property) not considered self-employment earnings.

Single Member LLC or Sole Proprietorship

Salary deferral contribution to a Solo 401k in 2016 is 100% of the owner's self employment earnings up to the maximum of $18,000 or $24,000 if age 50 or older. Same as above. However, for the profit sharing contribution a single member LLC or Schedule C sole-proprietor must do an added calculation starting with earned income to determine their maximum contribution which, in effect, brings the maximum 25% of compensation limit down to 20% of earned income. This calculation can be found in IRS Pub 560, section 5. In general, compensation is your net earnings from self employment.

Non Roth and Roth Contributions

The employee contributions can be non Roth (pre-tax dollars) or Roth (post-tax dollars) however there is one limit per person for all types of elective deferrals. The 2016 maximum of $18,000 (or $24,000 if age 50 or older) can be split in any ratio between the Roth and non-Roth elective deferrals.

The employer contribution can only be non Roth (pre-tax dollars).

Asset and Creditor Protection

If you are a participant of a 401k plan and you declare bankruptcy, your 401k plan assets will be exempt from the bankruptcy proceedings and your 401k could not be attached to the bankruptcy estates creditors. This is true since ERISA qualified plans as well as Solo 401k plans are have full bankruptcy exemption.

Generally, the pension, profit-sharing, or section 401k plans are generally safe from creditor claims both inside and outside of bankruptcy. However, Department of Labor Regulations have held that a plan that benefits only an owner (and/or an owner's spouse) are not ERISA plans (thus voiding the anti-alienation protections generally given to ERISA plans) and therefore Solo 401k plans protections are govern by state law when outside the bankruptcy context. Many states exempt the Solo 401k plan from creditors but you need to contact a competent attorney to find out for sure.

Chapter 7:
Self Directed SEP IRA

Simplified Employee Pension Plans (SEP IRA)

This plan is available to and designed for small business owners and self employed individuals. Typically, the businesses have 25 employees or less. SEP offers many of the tax benefits of the qualified plans like the 401k but it is less complicated and has lower administrative expenses.

- SEP contributions are tax deductible.
- SEP contributions are discretionary and can be up to 25% of earnings (up to $53,000 in 2016).
- All employer contributions are made to IRAs for the benefit of the eligible employees and are 100% immediately vested.
- Contributions and earnings grow tax-deferred until the money is withdrawn by the participant.
- Employer contributions are deductible business expenses.

- Plans are easy to set up and administer, with minimum paperwork and no complex IRS reporting requirements.

Eligibility

Any employer may establish a plan, even if there is only one employee. The employer can be a corporation, partnership or self-employed individual. Spouses may also participate as long as they are employed by the company and meet the income requirements. The employees must meet all of the following requirements:

- Worked for the business for at least 3 of the past 5 years
- Be at least 21 years old
- Earn the $600 annual minimum required compensation

SEP IRA Rules

In a SEP retirement plan, you are contributing to a Traditional IRA for yourself and your employees. You have the ability to choose the percentage of contribution (0-25% of earned income) for you and your employees. The percentage has to be the same for each employee and can only change once a year.

You can rollover or transfer an existing employer plan like a 401k, a pension plan or another SEP into a Self Directed SEP IRA.

Things to Note

- A SEP can be set up for a person's business even if he or she participates in another employer's retirement plan.
- The annual contribution an employer can make is the lesser of $53,000 for 2016 or 25% of the employee's compensation (for self employed the overall contribution limit is 20% of net profit of company – see IRS Pub. 560 for details).
- A SEP IRA must be setup for each employee and the IRA is owned and controlled by the employee and the employer sends the SEP contributions to the financial institution where the SEP IRA is maintained.
- Employer SEP contributions do not affect the amount a participant can contribute to an IRA. So, assuming the SEP IRA permits non-SEP contributions, regular IRA contributions can be made by the participant to his or her SEP IRA, up to the maximum annual limit (for 2016, $5,500 if under age 50 and $6,500 if 50 or over).

- Contributions must be made for each eligible employee in a SEP, even if over age 70 1/2.
- Contributions are not required to be made every year. However, in years contributions are made to the SEP they must be made to the SEP IRAs of all eligible employees.
- Employer receives a tax break and 100% of funds deposited are tax deductible.

Chapter 8:
Self Directed SIMPLE IRA

Savings Incentive Match Plans for Employees (SIMPLE IRA)

A SIMPLE IRA is a retirement plan for small businesses with 100 or fewer employees that have no other qualified plans. SIMPLE IRA is set up by an employer. The employee is responsible for contributions, all of which can be withheld from paychecks and directly deposited.

With a SIMPLE IRA, the employee is doing nearly all of the funding, and the employee is the one who gets the big tax break. An employee can only contribute up to $12,500 annually as of 2016. The limit goes up to $15,500 if the individual is 50 or older. Therefore, with a SIMPLE IRA, you can contribute more than with an individual IRA plans.

An employer can only contribute a small amount relative to the employee's income up to 3 percent of employee's compensation. The employer is responsible to match only if the employee contributes funds first. In a second option, an employer can simply contribute 2 percent whether or not the employee makes contributions. Based on these figures, it is obvious the contribution limits for the SIMPLE IRA are much lower than those for the SEP IRA. With a SIMPLE plan, contributions are tax deductible and tax deferred until withdrawn.

Points to Consider

- The company must either match participant contributions (dollar for dollar up to 3% of pay) or make a contribution of 2% of pay for all eligible participants.
- Contributions are 100% immediately vested.
- Certain notices must be provided annually to eligible employees.
- Employer match portion is a tax deductible business expense.
- Plans are low cost and easy to set up and administer with no complex IRS reporting requirements.

One other potentially important difference between a SEP and a SIMPLE plan is that, should you have to make an early withdrawal from the plan within two years of the plan's inception date, you will be penalized more in a SIMPLE IRA than you would be if it were a SEP IRA (25% penalty for a SIMPLE as compared to 10% penalty for a SEP).

Contributions by the employer to SIMPLE plans must be made by the employer's tax filing deadline, including valid extensions, for the employer to deduct contributions for that tax year.

Comparing SEP versus SIMPLE

	SEP IRA	***SIMPLE IRA***
Good for whom?	Self employed individuals with no employees or small business with less than 25 employees with certain compensation.	Small business employers with less than 100 employees and no other plan in place.
What are the main features?	No annual funding required. No IRS reporting requirements. Easy to administer. Employer must contribute to eligible employees accounts in year that plan is funded	No IRS reporting requirements. Largely funded by employee contributions. Limited employer contribution required. Easy to administer.

What are the tax benefits?	Contributions are generally tax deductible to the employer. Investment earnings grow tax deferred.	Contributions made by the employer and employee are tax deductible. Employee contributions are made on pre-tax basis and earnings grow tax deferred.
Can you take an early withdrawal?	Withdrawals prior to age 59½ are permitted, but may be subject to a 10% penalty plus ordinary income taxes.	Withdrawals prior to age 59½ are permitted, but may be subject to a 10% penalty plus ordinary income taxes. If this withdrawal occurs within the first 2 years of participation, the 10% penalty is increased to 25%.
What are the contribution limits?	Up to 25% of employee's compensation (up to $53,000 for 2016) or 20% of self employed individuals based on net earnings. All contributions are from the employer.	There are two options for employers. First option, match up to 3% or $12,500 whichever is less. Second option; contribute 2% of employee's compensation. Employee can contribute up to

		$12,500 for 2016 or $15,500 if 50+.
What are the age restrictions?	May exclude employees under age 21	None

Chapter 9: Business Acquisitions Solutions

Many business owners have been using retirement funds to acquire or invest in a business. Many people are getting downsized and want to start a new business but don't have the funds sitting in cash. Therefore, many are turning to the method known as ROBS (Rollover as Business Start-Up). ROBS are designed to allow individuals to use their existing retirement accounts for funding new businesses without first paying taxes on the distributions.

The IRS did concede that ROBS are not considered abusive tax avoidance transactions, but the IRS has branded such arrangements as "questionable." Before going into the reasons why, you need to get an overview of how the process works. But first, let's try to understand why someone would even consider such a plan. Below are the advantages claimed by the companies setting up these plans.

Advantages of This Funding Strategy

- An all cash purchase of a business eliminates the need for debt financing
- The ability to use your retirement to acquire a new business or grow an existing business tax free or tax deferred.
- Funds can be used as a down payment to secure additional financing
- Profits enjoy tax advantaged status by being directed back to your retirement plan
- As an owner of the business, you may draw a salary and receive benefits

Investing in your own business venture can get tricky since the IRS prohibits certain self dealing transactions between an IRA and any "disqualified person" (discussed in Chapter 3). While the IRS does not ban investments in a private company, the owner of an IRA and his/her direct relatives must own less than 50% of that company. The exception seems to be when you are starting a new venture and at the point when you are starting the business you don't yet own any of it. Therefore, you can use IRA funds, theoretically in unlimited amounts, for the startup financing.

The self dealing rules create additional complications if you're planning to work for your business, since you can't set your own pay. One idea is to set up a limited liability company, owned 90% by the IRA and the other 10% owned by an outsider who is the manager. That outsider can then hire the person(s) whose IRA owns 90% to run the business and the outsider sets their compensation--a key to making this kosher.

From all the reading I have done on the subject, it seems as if the IRS does scrutinize these transactions closely and that each plan is looked at on a case by case basis for compliance. Anyone considering a business acquisition using this strategy MUST work with a team of tax and ERISA attorneys to ensure the structure satisfies the IRS and ERISA rules and procedures. Reputable brokers provide written guarantees that they will fight the IRS on their dime if the IRS ever challenges the client's transactions. An additional protection would be to get an outside tax accountant or lawyer to look at the setup and to privately apply to the IRS for a favorable opinion letter or determination letter.

In summary, I am not saying that ROBS plans are illegal or do not potentially follow IRS regulations. However, many of these plans (in the opinion of the IRS) have not been established correctly and have potential, serious flaws in both design and execution. I am writing this to educate you on the concept of ROBS plans since you will hear and read about these plans in books and on the internet. Bottom line “buyer beware.”

A ROBS Plan Example

So, let’s take an example of a typical ROBS plan as explained by the IRS.

“A new business owner first creates a shell C corporation with created stock, but not issued. After incorporation, the newly created shell corporation adopts a retirement plan (typically a pre-approved plan), with a provision allowing 100% of the plan assets attributable to rollovers to be invested in employer stock. Next, the business owner either rolls over or executes a direct transfer of the proceeds from an existing tax deferred account, such as a 401k plan with a former employer, to the newly created ROBS plan. Once the rollover or direct transfer is complete, the business owner directs the shell corporation to issue all of its capital stock, and then transfer the stock to the ROBS plan in exchange for the proceeds held in the rollover account. After the transfer, the shell corporation has adequate capital to pursue business opportunities and the ROBS plan has capital stock in the corporation equal in value to the amount of the funds transferred. And, because all of the shell corporation’s stock has been allocated to the business owner’s ROBS plan account, any future employees or beneficiaries will not be able to invest in employer stock, barring a recapitalization." The IRS goes on to state that "the business owner has used rollover proceeds to indirectly start up or acquire a business while avoiding taxes on the transaction."

IRS Newsletter

In the fall 2010, the IRS published "Retirement News for Employers" newsletter which expressed concern that the promoters of these types of transactions do not have the expertise to develop structures that are fully compliant with IRS and ERISA rules and regulations. The IRS added that a large percentage of the transactions they reviewed were not compliant.

The IRS explained their concern by saying "A ROBS plan is an arrangement in which business owners use their retirement funds to pay for new business start-up costs. ROBS plans, while not considered abusive tax avoidance transactions, are questionable because they may solely benefit one individual — the individual who rolls over his existing retirement funds to the ROBS plan in a tax-free transaction. The ROBS plan then uses the rollover assets to purchase the stock of the new business."

The IRS memorandum dated October 1, 2008 said that ROBS transactions may violate law in several regards. First, this scheme might create a prohibited transaction between the plan and its sponsor. Second, this plan may not satisfy the benefits, rights and features requirement of the regulations. The primary utility of the arrangement may only be available to the business's principal individual.

The IRS concluded by saying "Specific facts will need to be evaluated on a case by case basis in order to make a proper determination as to whether these plans operationally comply with established law and guidance".

Many people that setup these plans say they have an IRS determination letter to assure them that the IRS approves of the ROBS arrangement. However, the IRS says in their newsletter "Determination letters do not give plan sponsors protection from incorrectly applying the plan's terms or from operating the plan in a discriminatory manner. When a plan sponsor administers a plan in a way that results in prohibited discrimination or engages in prohibited transactions, it can result in plan disqualification and adverse tax consequences to the plans sponsor and its participants."

The other thing that stood out when reading these IRS publications is that some promoters may not provided the best information to their clients. The IRS says "Many ROBS sponsors do not understand that a qualified plan is a separate entity with its own set of requirements. Some promoters incorrectly advised sponsors that they don't have to file an annual return because of an exception in the Form 5500-EZ instructions. IRS notes that the exception applies where plan assets are less than a specified dollar amount and the plan covers only an individual or an individual and his/her spouse....this filing exception doesn't apply to a ROBS plan and the annual Form 5500 or 5500-EZ is still required."

Some other problems with ROBS which were addressed in the IRS publication were:

1. **Amending the Plan** — The IRS notes that after the ROBS plan sponsor purchases the new company's employer stock with the rollover funds, the plan sponsor amends the plan to prevent other participants from purchasing stock.

2. **Exclusion** — The IRS states that, "If the sponsor amends the plan to prevent other employees from participating after the determination letter is issued, this may violate the Code qualification requirements."

3. **Promoter Fees** – The IRS believes that where fees have been paid to a promoter of such ROBS plans with transferred assets, a prohibited transaction may arise.

4. **Valuation of assets** – The IRS takes the position that, "Setting the value of the corporation's stock at the value of the transferred plan assets may be a prohibited transaction, especially where the stock value was set without an adequately supported appraisal of the stock's value."

5. **Failure to issue 1099-R** - the IRS addresses the failure to issue a Form 1099-R, Distributions From Pensions, Annuities, Retirement or Profit-Sharing Plans, IRAs, Insurance Contracts, etc., when the assets are rolled over into the ROBS plan.

Bottom line is that you must be aware of the complexities of acquiring a business using your retirement funds. Please take the time to read and get the best tax attorney money can buy to make sure your plan is compliant with the IRS.

Health/Education Plans

Chapter 10:
Self Directed HSA
(Health Savings Account)

A health savings account (HSA) is a tax exempt trust or custodial account that you set up with a qualified HSA trustee to pay or reimburse certain medical expenses you incur. You must be an eligible individual to qualify for an HSA. You can setup a Self Directed HSA with a custodian who allows you to invest in alternative assets.

No permission or authorization from the IRS is necessary to establish an HSA. When you set up an HSA, you will need to work with a trustee. A qualified HSA trustee can be a bank, an insurance company, or anyone already approved by the IRS to be a trustee of individual retirement arrangements (IRAs). The HSA can be established through a trustee that is different from your health plan provider.

Who Is Eligible?

The requirements to qualify for a HSA account are as follows:

- You are not enrolled in Medicare.
- You have no other health care coverage except what is permitted.
- You are covered under a high deductible health plan (HDHP – see IRS Publication 969 for more information)
- You cannot be claimed as a dependent on someone else's tax return.

For 2016, a HDHP (high deductible health insurance plan) means a plan that has an annual deductible of not less than $1,300 for individuals (or $2,600 for families) and has required out-of-pocket maximums of not more than $6,550 for individuals (or $13,100 for families).

What Are The Benefits?

- Enrolling in the mandatory high deductible health plans will reduce your monthly premium costs.
- Contributions are tax deductible (subject to limitations).
- Contributions can be invested in the same way as a Self Directed IRA, with the possibility of accumulating tax free or tax deferred profits in investments that you know best.
- Contributions can be carried over from one tax year to the next—forget about the "use it

or lose it" requirement imposed upon flexible spending accounts.

- If money is withdrawn to pay for qualified medical expenses, the distribution is tax free.
- Earnings on amounts in an HSA are not included in your income while held in the HSA.

Who Can Contribute To HSA And What Are The Limits?

For employer sponsored HSA, the employee and employer may contribute to the employee's HSA in the same year. For an HSA established by a self-employed individual, the individual can contribute. Family members or any other person may also make contributions on behalf of an eligible individual.

The contribution limits depend on the type of HDHP the person obtains, your age, the date you became eligible and the date you ceased to be eligible. In 2016, if you have self only HDHP coverage, you can contribute up to $3,350 and if you have family HDHP coverage you can contribute up to $6,750. The catch up provision for those 55 or older remains at $1000. There are some variations for those who were not an eligible individual the entire year or changed their type of coverage during the year. The details are in IRS Publication 969.

What Are The Distributions Rules?

You will generally pay medical expenses during the year without being reimbursed by your HDHP until you reach the annual deductible for the plan. When you pay medical expenses during the year that are not reimbursed by your HDHP, you can ask the trustee of your HSA to send you a distribution from your HSA. You can receive tax free distributions from your HSA to pay or be reimbursed for qualified medical expenses you incur after you establish the HSA. If you receive distributions for other reasons, the amount you withdraw will be subject to income tax and may be subject to an additional 10% penalty. You do not have to make distributions from your HSA each year.

What If I (The HSA Holder) Dies?

When you setup a HSA you will choose a beneficiary. If the designated beneficiary is your spouse, then the HSA will be treated as your spouse's HSA after your death. If your spouse is not the designated beneficiary of your HSA then your account stops being a HSA and the HSA becomes taxable to the beneficiary in the year in which you die. If your estate is the beneficiary then the value of the HSA is included on your final income tax return.

Chapter 11: Self Directed CESA (Coverdell Education Savings Account)

The CESA allows individuals to invest funds for educational purposes. This trust or custodial account is created for the purpose of paying qualified education expenses of the designated beneficiary. The designated beneficiary must be under 18 years of age or a special needs beneficiary. This benefit can be for elementary, secondary or higher education expenses. Again, you can setup a Self Directed CESA which allows you to invest in alternative assets like real estate, notes, gold, private lending, etc.

If your modified adjusted gross income (MAGI) is less than $110,000 (or $220,000 if filing a joint return), then you may be able to establish a Coverdell ESA to finance the educational expenses of a certain beneficiary. The total contributions for the beneficiary in any year cannot exceed $2,000 and are nondeductible. Another thing to note is that the money in the account cannot be invested in life insurance.

Contributions and Distributions

Any individual can contribute to a CESA as long as they make under the MAGI limits described above. Organizations such as corporations and trust can also contribute with no requirement that the organizations income be below a certain limit. Contributions to a CESA are not tax deductible, but money left in the account grows tax free until distributed. In addition, distributions are tax free as long as the distributions did not exceed the qualified education expenses for the year. Contributions cannot be made after the beneficiary reaches age 18 (unless special needs situation) and must be made before the contributor's tax return due date.

The balance of the account must be distributed within 30 days after either the beneficiary's death or when the beneficiary reaches 30, whichever occurs earlier.

Finally, contributions can be made to several Coverdell Education Savings Accounts for the same designated beneficiary provided that the total contributions are not more than the limits for a year. If a parent, a grandmother and aunt each setup a

CESA for a child then the total contributions cannot be more than $2,000. For example, if the parents contributed $2,000 to one of child's CESA, then the grandmother and aunt could not contribute that year to the other CESAs.

What Higher Education Expenses Are Qualified?

Any expenses related to the enrollment or attendance at a qualified college, university, vocational school, or other eligible postsecondary school. The following expenses if required for enrollment or attendance are typically covered such as tuition, fees, books, supplies, equipment, etc. Expenses for room and board are covered for students who are enrolled at least half time.

What Elementary And Secondary Education Expenses Are Qualified?

The expenses covered are similar to those described above for the higher education with a few additions. Academic tutoring, uniforms, certain transportation, computer technology, internet access and related services are all qualified educational expenses when used by the beneficiary during the years in elementary or secondary school.

RESOURCES

Self Directed IRA Custodians

CAMA Self Directed IRA
Blue Bell, PA
215-283-2868
CamaPlan.com

Equity Trust Company
Westlake, OH
888-382-4727
TrustETC.com

Entrust Group
Oakland, CA
800-392-9653
TheEntrustGroup.com

Lincoln Trust Company
Denver, CO
800-831-8675
Ltretire.com

Millennium Trust Company
Oak Brook, IL
800-258-7878
MTrustCompany.com

Pensco Trust Company
San Francisco, CA
866-818-4472
Pensco.com

Polycomp Trust Company
Roseville, CA
800-952-8800
Polycomp.net

Self Directed IRA Services
Austin, TX
866-928-9394
SDIRAservices.com

Quest IRA
Houston, TX
855-386-4727
Questira.com

Sunwest Trust, Inc.
Albuquerque, NM
800-642-7167
SunWestTrust.com

IRA LLC and/or Solo 401k Facilitators

IRA Financial Group
New York, NY
800-472-0646
IraFinancialGroup.com

Safeguard Financial
Lake Oswego, OR
877-229 9763
Ira123.com

Guidant Financial Services
Bellevue, WA
888-472-4455
GuidantFinancial.com

IRA Advantage
Portland, OR
800-475-1031
IraAdvantage.net

IRA Checkbook
Charleston, SC
800-530-8522
IraCheckBook.com

Made in the USA
Monee, IL
08 November 2026

67967621R00059